earth smart crafts

transform toss-away items into fun accessories, gifts, room décor & more!

by Carrie Anton

★ American Girl®

Published by American Girl Publishing, Inc.

Copyright © 2009 by American Girl, LLC

Questions or comments? Call 1-800-845-0005,
visit our Web site at americangirl.com, or write to
Customer Service, American Girl, 8400 Fairway Place, Middleton, WI 53562-0497.

Printed in China

09 10 11 12 13 LEO 10 9 8 7 6 5 4 3 2 1

All American Girl marks are trademarks of American Girl, LLC.

Editorial Development: Carrie Anton

Art Direction and Design: Lisa Wilber, Camela Decaire

Production: Kendra Schluter, Sarah Boecher, Julie Kimmell, Jeannette Bailey, Judith Lary

Photography: Radlund Photography

Stylist: Carrie Anton

Cataloging-in-Publication Data available from the Library of Congress.

Dear Reader,

Now you can **reuse, recycle, and RE-CREATE!** The crafts in this book offer **clever ways** to take items usually tossed in the trash and make trendy pieces to wear, dress up your space, and give as gifts.

When it comes to giving **Mother Nature** a helping hand, one girl really can **make a difference.** And this book shows you how to do it with **style!**

Your friends at American Girl

table of contents

getting started

keep it safe

Please read through the directions carefully. The supplies you'll need are listed with each craft. Be sure to gather all of your supplies before you begin.

Always ask an adult to help when you see this hand 🖐 or when a project seems too difficult to complete on your own.

When working with messy supplies such as paint and glue, be sure to cover your work-space with newspaper. Always keep craft supplies out of the reach of small children.

special craft supplies

scissors

For projects requiring fabric to be cut, special **fabric scissors** may be necessary. Since these scissors are sharper than those used for paper, always have an adult help you with them.

tape

You may need different types of tape, depending on the project you're working on.

- **Traditional clear tape** is found at most stores, including craft stores and office supply stores.

- **Double-stick tape** is sticky on both sides so that you can attach two surfaces together without having to make a loop of tape. Double-stick tape is less messy than glue, but either one can usually be used.

- **Packaging tape** is a wider and stronger clear tape used for assembling and closing boxes. It is also a great craft supply for taping large sections together.

- **Duct tape** is a super-strong tape that comes in different colors.

glue

Always use **craft glue** unless a project specifically calls for another kind. Craft glue cleans up easily with water and holds different materials together well.

Other projects call for using a **glue stick** or **Glue Dots,** both of which you can find at craft stores.

Additional supplies you may need are listed below. Even though most are available at craft stores, look around your house, at garage sales, and at thrift stores to see what can be reused. Remember, the point is to recycle!

- brads
- chenille stems
- craft paint
- decoupage glue
- embroidery hoops
- foam paintbrushes
- jewelry hardware
- markers
- paper punches
- safety pins

gathering found objects

Being a crafty green girl is less about what you make and more about what you use to make it. Almost anyone can make a bracelet or necklace with supplies from the craft store, but a clever and environmentally concerned person will look for ways to reduce trash and reuse it to make something really cool.

That doesn't mean you should string a stinky food can around your neck and call it fashion! But if you give that can a good cleaning, cover it in some wrapping paper left over from your birthday, and place it on your desk, you'll have a pretty holder for loose paper clips and small erasers.

why use trash for crafts?

The better question is "Why not?" Everyone needs to do her part to help protect the earth's natural resources. One way to do that is to dump less in the trash. Before you head for the garbage can, look at what you're about to toss and see if you can come up with another way to use it.

no dumpster diving necessary

All of the crafts in this book require reusing something that you might have normally thrown away. But that doesn't mean you should dig through your neighbor's trash bins on garbage day hoping to find some gems. Instead, work with your parents to set up multiple recycle bins—some for items you're looking to collect and another for items that can hit the curb.

You can even turn collecting your trash "craft" supplies into a craft project itself by making decorative labels for your recycle bins.

Bags

Paper

Fabric

save-the-earth styles

dress up your look with cast-offs cool enough to wear

pretty in plastic

To wear, ask a parent to tie the ends together behind your neck, or use jewelry hardware to hold together.

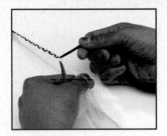

1. From one or more plastic bags, cut three 1-inch-thick strips. Each strip will be a big ring. Snip the end of each ring so that it's a flat strip.

2. Tie all three strips together with a knot at one end. Braid the strips together and tie a knot to secure the ends.

3. Decorate a rim tag with a sticker, silk flower, brad, or small image cut from a magazine. String the ring onto the braided cord.

funky felted belt

You will need:

- 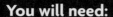 an adult's help
- a wool sweater that was accidentally shrunk in the wash
- fabric scissors
- a sewing needle
- thread
- buttons

1. Cut the band off the bottom of a sweater. Cut one end of the band to create a long strip.

2. Decorate your belt with felt shapes cut from the body of the sweater. Sew on the shapes using buttons.

To wear, wrap the belt around your waist and tie the ends together.

wrist warmer

To wear, button the ends around your wrist. Pair up the Wrist Warmer with the Funky Felted Belt for a coordinating look!

1. Cut the cuff band off one shrunken wool sweater sleeve. Cut one end of the band to create a flat strip.

2. Measure the strip around your wrist and mark where it overlaps by 1 inch. Remove from your wrist and cut off the excess.

3. Sew one or two buttons along one edge.

4. Once your buttons are attached, mark on the other end of the strip where the buttons line up. Ask an adult for help cutting a small opening for each button.

pressed-plastic pouch

You will need:

-  an adult's help
- 3 plastic shopping bags
- 2 pieces of poster board
- an ironing board
- an iron
- scissors
- tape
- a small paper punch
- brads

To use, put your money, coins and library card in your pouch for safekeeping.

16

Warning: Do not touch the iron directly to the plastic. Use the poster boards to prevent ruining your iron.

1. ✋ On an ironing board, sandwich the plastic bags between the poster board pieces. With help from an adult, use a medium-temperature iron on the poster board to bond the bags together.

2. Continue ironing the poster board, letting it cool every few minutes so that it can be flipped over and ironed on the other side. Check after each cooling to see if all the pieces have bonded together.

3. Once the plastic has bonded and cooled, cut the plastic into a rectangle. Fold one short end three-fourths of the way up. Use a piece of removable tape to temporarily hold it in place.

4. On the folded section, punch holes up both sides. Use brads to hold the sides together.

5. On the underside of the top flap, tape on a loop made from a leftover plastic strip. Attach a brad in the middle of the pouch for a closure.

17

wrapped-up beads

To wear, make enough straw beads to string on a chain, ribbon, or cord with other decorative beads. Tie the ends, or use jewelry hardware to close.

1. Using the pattern on page 62 for each bead, trace and cut out one triangle from wrapping paper.

2. Cover the back side of the triangle with glue. Place the wide end on the straw and tightly roll the paper.

3. Snip off the ends of the straw so that only the wrapping paper shows. Repeat all steps to make more beads.

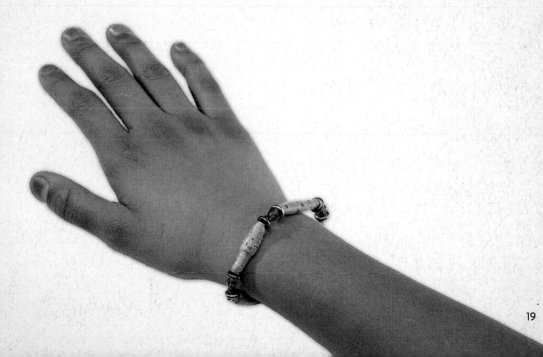

a refreshing bracelet

You will need:

- 👐 an adult's help
- 15-20 pull tabs taken from the tops of soda cans (ask an adult to remove the tabs so that there are no sharp edges)
- 2 pieces of 18-inch-long thin ribbon

To wear, wrap around your wrist and have another person tie the ends.

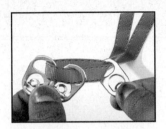

1. String one piece of ribbon through two side-by-side pull tabs.

2. String both ends of the ribbon from front to back through a third pull tab.

3. Take one end of the ribbon and string it through a fourth tab from back to front.

4. Continue stringing the same ribbon end from back to front through the top pull tab.

5. Continue this pattern, adding tabs in twos as you go.

6. Weave a second piece of ribbon through the other openings. Tie knots to secure both sides.

a stretchy headband

 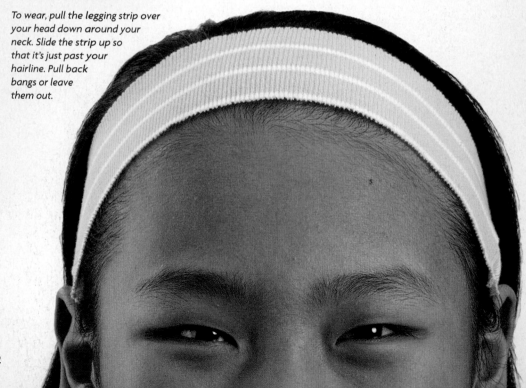
1. Ask Mom or Dad if it's O.K. to recycle an old pair of leggings.

2. With help from an adult, cut a 2-inch strip at the widest part of the leg—or the part that will fit best around your head.

To wear, pull the legging strip over your head down around your neck. Slide the strip up so that it's just past your hairline. Pull back bangs or leave them out.

22

button bonanza

You will need:
- a plain barrette
- Glue Dots or craft glue
- various buttons

1. Decorate a plain barrette by gluing on layers of buttons. Recycle buttons by asking your dad if he has a stained or too-small button-down shirt from which you can snip buttons. Or search garage sales for old shirts with pretty buttons.

2. If using craft glue, let each layer of buttons dry before adding more.

To wear, hold the sides of your hair back with your new barrette, or use it to dress up a plain ponytail.

wearable lids

You will need:

- 👋 an adult's help
- scissors
- 3 to 5 thin plastic container lids from peanuts, potato chips, yogurt, etc.
- small and large paper punches in different shapes
- glue (optional)
- ribbon (optional)
- jewelry hardware (optional)

1. Cut the rim edge off the lid. With help from an adult, punch out different shapes from the remaining plastic.

2. Be creative and find fun ways to pair up the shapes using glue, jewelry hardware, and ribbon.

3. For earrings, punch small holes in a shape for earring studs to fit through, or hang shapes from dangling earring wires.

Tip:

If clear lids are all you can find, use the paper punches and scrap wrapping paper to give your jewelry some color. Just glue the punched paper to the punched plastic!

a fashionable fold-up

You will need:
- lots of 2-by-4-inch strips of old catalogues or magazines
- regular tape
- packaging tape
- ribbon or cord

How to fold:

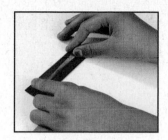

1. Fold each piece of paper lengthwise, and then fold one side up to meet the center fold.

2. Fold the other side in to meet the center fold. You don't need to fold any further for the middle pieces of the row.

3. For the first and last pieces of a row, complete steps 1 and 2 and then bend the folded-up piece in half width-wise. Fold in each end to meet the center fold.

How to make rows:

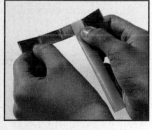

1. Letting the first strip flop open, place the end of the second strip so that it makes a "T" before the last crease in the first strip.

2. Fold the ends of the first strip in half toward the middle.

3. Fold the second strip up and over the back of the first strip.

Turn the page for more steps.

How to make rows, continued:

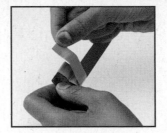

4. Line up a third strip under the first so that it is behind the second piece. Fold the short end around the second strip.

5. Fold the second strip up and over the first and third strips.

6. Tuck the end of the second strip behind the third strip. Repeat with more strips across the row.

How to connect the rows:

7. Tape down the end of the last strip in the back of the row.

1. Line up the rows and use regular tape to hold them in place. When all rows are in place, you should have a rectangle.

2. Fold up the sides in the direction you were adding rows to create a pouch.

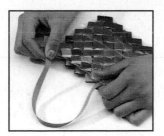

3. Cover the whole pouch with packaging tape to hold the sides together and protect the paper.

4. Decorate with additional embellishments, such as a ribbon or cord for a handle.

reuse, recycle, redecorate

reuse simple stuff to give your room a redo

cd nameplate

You will need:

- scissors
- brown paper bags
- one empty CD case for each letter of your name
- leftover wrapping paper
- glue
- binder clips

1. Cut out squares of brown paper bags using the inside covers of music CDs as templates.

2. On wrapping paper, draw and cut out each letter of your name. Glue the letters to the paper bag squares. Once dry, slip the letters into the CD cases. Use binder clips to hang the cases.

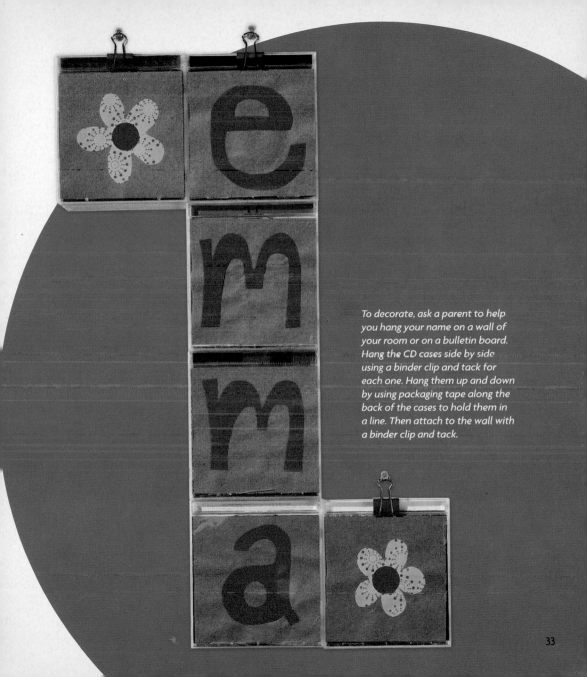

To decorate, ask a parent to help you hang your name on a wall of your room or on a bulletin board. Hang the CD cases side by side using a binder clip and tack for each one. Hang them up and down by using packaging tape along the back of the cases to hold them in a line. Then attach to the wall with a binder clip and tack.

T-shirt tiles

You will need:
-  an adult's help
- an embroidery hoop
- an old T-shirt with a fun print or design
- fabric scissors

Find a place on the T-shirt that you'd like to use as wall art. Place the smaller of the two hoop pieces under this spot. Place the larger hoop on top so that the T-shirt is between the two pieces. Tighten the embroidery hoop to close it. Pull the T-shirt taut so that no ripples appear. With help from an adult, cut off the excess T-shirt fabric close to the back of the hoop.

Tip:
Using a T-shirt with a pocket for this project gives you a cute place to display a small silk flower or tiny toy stuffed animal.

To decorate your room, ask a parent to help you hang up your new wall art. You could even make a memory wall of all your old T-shirts.

book shirt

You will need:

- 🖐 an adult's help
- fabric scissors
- an old T-shirt
- a ruler
- a book to be covered
- a pencil
- packaging tape
- colored duct tape
- stickers or rub-ons

Tip:

When you're through with
the book, remove the T-shirt cover
to reuse on a similar-sized book.

1. With help from an adult, cut open a T-shirt. Place the book on the material and open the cover. Measure and mark 2 inches from all sides.

2. Remove the book, and use a ruler to connect the lines so that they make a rectangle. Cut out the rectangle.

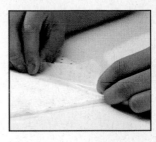

3. Fold over 2 inches of the top and bottom edges and tape down. Lay the book back on the material, which should now be the same height as the book.

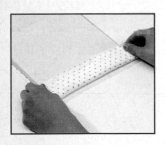

4. Fold the ends over each cover.

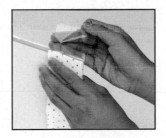

5. Tape the corners of the fabric, making sure that the packaging tape doesn't touch the book.

6. Hide the packaging tape using colored duct tape. Decorate the duct tape with stickers or rub-ons.

give-a-hoot scratch pad

You will need:

- scissors
- a cereal box
- patterns on pages 60–61
- glue
- a stack of scrap paper that is blank on one side
- a pencil
- a paper punch
- brads

1. Using the patterns on pages 60 and 61, trace and cut out 2 large circles and a triangle from a cereal box. Cut out the remaining shapes on these pages from scrap paper. Glue together your shapes to make an owl. Use the large circle template again to cut out your scratch-pad paper.

2. Punch holes in the cardboard covers and use them as guides to make a mark on each piece of scratch paper. Punch holes where marked. Line up all the sheets so that the blank sides are facing front. Put on the front and back covers and secure them with brads.

Tip:

Junk mail is a great resource for scrap paper.

jewelry drawers

1. Cut a strip of paper as wide as a matchbox.

2. Tape one end of the strip to the bottom of one matchbox, and tightly wrap the paper around the outside. Trim the excess paper, and tape down the second end. Repeat this step with the two other boxes.

3. Once the boxes are wrapped, glue them so that they are stacked on top of one another. Let dry.

4. Ask an adult to poke a spare earring through the front of each "drawer." Secure the earring by putting the back on to the post.

You will need:
- 🖐 an adult's help
- 3 empty matchboxes
- leftover wrapping paper or scraps of craft paper
- tape
- glue
- 3 spare stud earrings

Store your earrings in the matchbox drawers to keep them together in one place.

paper-perfect desk cup

You will need:

- scissors
- old magazines or catalogues
- double-stick tape
- a small jar, can, or container

To use, fill with loose items on your desk, such as paper clips, erasers, or rubber bands. Decorate larger jars in the same way to make matching containers to hold your pens and pencils.

1. To make one accordion-folded strip, cut two ¼- or ½-inch-wide strips from scrap magazine or catalogue pages (the longer the strips, the better). Lay one end of one strip on top of one end of the other strip so that two strips make a corner.

2. Fold the first strip over the second so that you see the back of both pieces.

3. Next, fold the second strip over the first. Repeat to the ends. Place double-stick tape on the jar or container, and stick one end of the accordion fold to it. Stretch and wrap the strip around the jar. Use another piece of double-stick tape to hold the other end. Repeat until the whole jar is covered.

cd-case cubbies

Use these to display knickknacks or to organize lightweight objects, such as other CDs.

1. Open 2 CD cases. Spread glue or use Glue Dots along one lip of each case. Glue the ends together, forming a square. Let dry. Repeat with another 2 CD cases.

2. Remove the tops from two CD cases. Glue the bottom to the back of each opening.

3. Cut out squares of paper using the CD's inside cover as a template. Use these sheets as decoration inside your cubbies.

Tip:
Complete steps 1–3 to make as many cubes as needed. Stack and glue them as you go to create your own unique structure.

regift it!

give old objects new life as great gifts

roller coasters

You will need:

- old catalogues or magazines
- double-stick tape
- an empty cereal box
- a pencil
- scissors

Gift idea: A set of four coasters makes a good gift for someone who likes to have guests.

1. Cut 2-inch-wide strips from scrap catalogue or magazine pages (the longer the strip, the better). Fold the strip in half lengthwise twice. Repeat to make several folded strips.

2. Tightly roll the first strip of paper. When the first strip is rolled, tape the second strip to the end of the first and continue rolling tightly. Continue adding strips until the circle is wide enough for a soda can to sit on. Use double-stick tape as you roll to help secure the strips. Decorate the outer edge with ribbon and double-stick tape.

3. Trace the shape of the coaster onto a cereal box, and cut out the shape. Attach the cardboard with double-stick tape to one side of the coaster to be the bottom.

sweet ornaments

You will need:

-  an adult's help
- a candy tin
- leftover wrapping or craft paper
- ribbon
- double-stick tape
- a photo

Remove the top from a clean candy tin. (If there are any rough edges, ask an adult to fold them in.) Decorate the inside using scrap wrapping paper, ribbon, double-stick tape, and a photo. Loop and tie or glue on a piece of ribbon. Let dry. Make a second ornament with the bottom of the tin.

Pretty Kitty

Gift idea: Add a picture of you and a friend for a personalized holiday gift.

tic-tac-toe to go

You will need:

- a candy tin
- leftover wrapping or craft paper
- a marker
- scissors
- double-stick tape or glue
- buttons
- adhesive magnet strips
- embellishments

Trace the bottom of a candy tin onto scrap paper and cut out. Draw on lines to create a tic-tac-toe board. Use double-stick tape or glue to attach the game board inside the tin. Cut magnet strips and attach to buttons. Keep the button magnets inside the tin to use as the Xs and Os. Decorate the outside of the tin with scrap paper, ribbons, and letters cut from magazines.

Gift idea: Give this game to a sibling. It will help you pass the time on long car trips.

sweater gift sacks

You will need:

- ⭐ an adult's help
- a wool sweater that was accidentally shrunk in the wash
- a large bowl
- a pencil
- scissors
- a large-eye sewing needle
- ribbon

Use a large bowl to trace and cut out a circle from the sweater. With help from an adult, thread a long piece of ribbon through a large-eye needle. Sew large stitches around the outside of the circle, letting a long length of ribbon hang from the first stitch. After the last stitch, pull the needle off the ribbon. Hold both ends of the ribbon in one hand and gather the edges to form a bag. Cut a small strip of the remaining sweater to make a handle for the bag. Sew on the handle.

Gift idea: Fill the bag with candy to make a sweet sweater treat for someone.

napkin wrappers

Coat the back of a piece of scrap wrapping paper with glue. Tightly wrap the paper around a cardboard tube. Let dry. Starting from the end, mark off every 2 inches on the wrapped tube. With help from an adult, use the scissors to cut where marked.

Tip:

Use coordinating papers to create a complete set of napkin rings when you don't have enough paper in one pattern.

Gift idea: Make a set of 8 for an aunt who loves to throw dinner parties.

picture-and-pencil holder

You will need:

- 👑 an adult's help
- a cleaned-out soup can
- a can opener
- paper
- scissors
- tape, double-stick tape, or glue
- ribbon (optional)

Ask a parent to smooth any rough edges of a cleaned-out soup can by running a can opener along the open edge. Using leftover wrapping paper or scraps of craft paper, cut a strip of paper that is as wide as the can. Tape one end of the strip to the back of the can, and tightly wrap the paper around the outside. Trim the excess paper and tape down the second end. To decorate the can, attach a scrap of ribbon with double-stick tape or glue.

Gift idea: Combine the pencil holder and magnets to make a gift for which you're sure to be remembered.

Tip:

Decorate the insides of two different types of metal bottle tops with photos and stickers. Glue old fridge magnets to the backs of the bottle tops and attach them to the can.

portable picture frame

You will need:

- scissors
- an empty CD case
- scrap wrapping paper
- double-stick tape
- a photo
- a piece of scrap ribbon
- a large Popsicle stick

Cut out a square of scrap paper using the inside cover of a music CD as a template. Use double-stick tape to attach a photo to this piece of paper. Slip the photo back into the CD case. Cover the title of the CD with ribbon. Use a large Popsicle stick to hold open the case and prop up the picture.

Gift idea: A picture of you will be a big hit with your mom or dad.

you and me

a tasty vase

Cut different-width strips of paper from a magazine or catalogue. Use a foam brush to coat the bottom section of a potato chip container with decoupage glue. Wrap the strips around the glue-coated section of the can. Repeat until the whole can is covered with paper. Then, put a coat of decoupage glue over the whole can. Decorate with paper shapes and more decoupage glue. Let dry.

Gift idea: To brighten someone's day, fill a thin glass vase with water and a flower, and place it inside the Tasty Vase.

two-card flip book

You will need:

- 2 playing cards (from a deck that is missing cards)
- a pencil
- scissors
- brown paper bags
- a paper hole punch
- ribbon
- craft glue
- a button
- a rubber band

1. Trace a playing card onto brown paper grocery bags as many times as you want pages for your book. Cut out the pages. Punch two holes in the end of one playing card. Line up the second playing card and mark the holes. Punch holes where marked. Repeat with each page cut out. Line up all of the holes and tie together with pieces of ribbon.

2. On the front cover, use a drop of craft glue to attach a button. On the back cover, punch a hole at the end opposite the ribbons. String a rubber band halfway through the hole. Then string the other half of the rubber band through the first half. Pull tight. Loop the rubber band around the button to hold the cover closed.

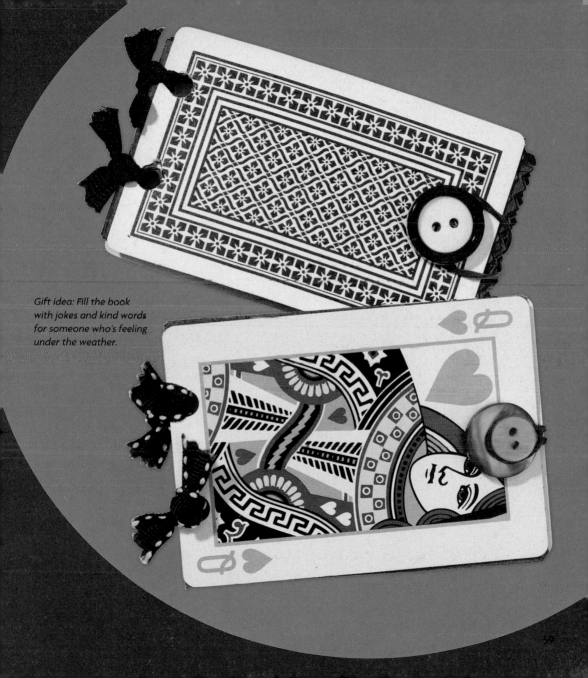

Gift idea: Fill the book with jokes and kind words for someone who's feeling under the weather.

patterns

Patterns on these two pages are for the Give-A-Hoot Scratch Pad on page 38.
To use, photocopy them at 100%.

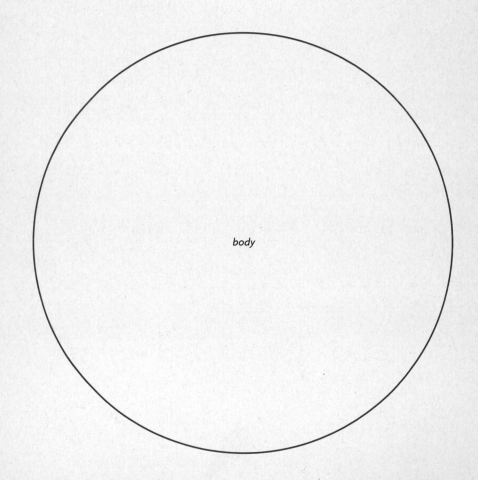

body

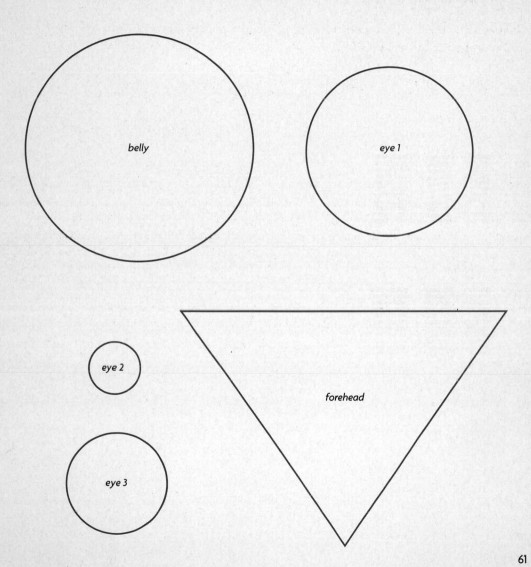

belly

eye 1

eye 2

eye 3

forehead

patterns

The pattern on this page is for the Wrapped-Up Beads on page 18.
To use, photocopy it at 150%.

Are you a green girl?

We want to know what kinds of things
you're doing to help recycle.

Write to:

Earth Smart Crafts Editor
American Girl
8400 Fairway Place
Middleton, WI 53562

Recycle This Book

Just like all of the toss-away items you've
turned into crafts, this book can be reused. When
you're done with it, pass it around to a group of
friends, donate it to a library, or make it part
of a book sale to benefit charity.

Here are some other American Girl books you might like:

❏ I read it.

❏ I read it.

❏ I read it.

❏ I read it.

❏ I read it.